First World War
and Army of Occupation
War Diary
France, Belgium and Germany

60 DIVISION
Headquarters, Branches and Services
Adjutant and Quarter-Master General
1 November 1915 - 31 December 1915

WO95/3026/4

The Naval & Military Press Ltd
www.nmarchive.com
Published in association with The National Archives

Published by

The Naval & Military Press Ltd

Unit 10 Ridgewood Industrial Park,
Uckfield, East Sussex,
TN22 5QE England
Tel: +44 (0) 1825 749494

www.naval-military-press.com

www.nmarchive.com

This diary has been reprinted in facsimile from the original. Any imperfections are inevitably reproduced and the quality may fall short of modern type and cartographic standards.

© Crown Copyright
Images reproduced by permission of The National Archives, London, England, 2015.

Contents

Document type	Place/Title	Date From	Date To
Heading	WO95/3026/4		
Heading	War Diary of D.A.Q.M.G. From December 1st 1915 To December 31st 1915		
War Diary		01/11/1915	31/12/1915

WO 95/30264

Confidential
War Diary
of
A.A.Q.M.G.

NOV 1915
From :- December 1st. 1915.
To :- December 31st. 1915.

Army Form C. 2118.

Winchester Branch
60 (Chatten/Severn)

WAR DIARY
or
INTELLIGENCE SUMMARY

(Erase heading not required.)

Instructions regarding War Diaries and Intelligence
Summaries are contained in F. S. Regs., Part II.
and the Staff Manual respectively. Title pages
will be prepared in manuscript.

Hour, Date, Place	Summary of Events and Information	Remarks and references to Appendices
November 1st.	III Army notified us that 3d per gallon extra might be paid for petrol where demanded. Orders received for Lieut. Tucker, D.A.D.O.S., to join Mediterranean Expeditionary Force. 2/6th R.F.A. moved from Camp to billets at Much Hadham.	
2nd.	2/5th R.F.A. moved from Camp to billets at Stansted. 3 Officers asked for as reinforcements from 2/19th Bn. London Regiment. 2/23rd Bn. London Regt. moved from Bishop's Stortford Camp to billets at Braintree. 2/7th R.F.A. moved from Camp to billets at Stansted.	
3rd.	All concerned notified that O.C. Brigades have power to interchange horses within their commands where they are unsuitably placed. 2/3rd Field Co. R.E. moved from Stansted Camp to billets at B. Stortford.	
4th.	Arrangements made for all remounts to be sent to Bishop's Stortford instead of the stations of Units. Instructions forwarded by III Army circulated re purchase of spare parts for Mechanical Transport. 2/22nd Bn. London Regt. moved from Bishop's Stortford Camp to billets at Dunmow. 2/24th Bn. London Regt. moved from Bishop's Stortford Camp to billets at Braintree. 2/4th Field Co. R.E. moved from Stansted Camp to billets at B. Stortford. Rev. J.E. Reilly (Wesleyan) appointed non-conformist Chaplain.	
5th.	The following appointed Civil Medical Practitioners from dates mentioned:- Dr. A. W. Ewing ... Oct. 27th 1915. Dr. H. E. Dickson ... Oct. 27th 1915. Dr. White ... Oct. 28th 1915. Dr. Caudwell ... Nov. 2nd 1915. Dr. Reckitt ... Nov. 2nd 1915. Dr. Huxtable ... Nov. 8th 1915. 1/6th Field Co. R.E. moved from Stansted Camp to billets at B. Stortford. 69th (East Anglian) Artillery left for Cambridge and are struck off the strength of the Division.	

Army Form C. 2118.

WAR DIARY
or
INTELLIGENCE SUMMARY (Sheet 2.)
(Erase heading not required.)

Instructions regarding War Diaries and Intelligence Summaries are contained in F. S. Regs., Part II. and the Staff Manual respectively. Title pages will be prepared in manuscript.

Hour, Date, Place		Summary of Events and Information	Remarks and references to Appendices
November	5th (Ctd)	Orders received for two Officers of the 2/19th Battn. London Regt. to proceed to Soton. Application made to appoint Capt. David Devis, Adjutant to the 2/13th London Regiment. Orders received to return to Colchester any accoutrements held on charge for use of draft overseas.	
	6th	Report of Inspector of Q.M.G.Services on 60th (London) Divl. Train forwarded. Capt. A.H.Crabbe, 2/23rd London Regt. appointed to act as A.P.M. temporarily. Two Officers asked for as reinforcements from each 2/6th, 2/7th and 2/8th F.A.Brigades. Application made to appoint Capt.Nox Adjutant of 2/23rd London Regiment. Rev.F.J.Newson appointed Church of England Chaplin. Dr.J.Atkinson (Jnr) appointed Civil Medical Practitioner.	
	7th	Return of Number of blankets on charge asked for in Divisional Orders. One Officer as reinforcement required from the 2/20th London Regt. Capt.G.S.F.Napier (G.S.02) proceeded to Godstone on duty. (returning on completion.)	
	8th	Return asked for from All Units stating that their Messing Accounts had been rendered to the Messing Auditor. Divisional Order stating that care was to be taken that no infected blankets etc. are put on rail by Units. G.O.C. addressed all Brigade and Divisional Troop Commanders and Staffs on discipline and interior economy.	
	9th	Orders received for three Regular M.M.P. Sergeants to return to Aldershot. Orders received for all Bands to be disbanded.	
	10th.	Report called for from all Units as to what arrangements they have made for Central Feeding. 50 G.S.Wagons arrived for distribution. Officer reinforcements from artillery to proceed to Southampton. Rev.L.M.Tenton appointed C.E.Chaplain. G.O.C. inspected the 180th Infantry Brigade. Transfers approved :- Major Sir C.P.V.Pole from 2nd to 3rd Line, 3/23rd London Regt. Temporary Major V.Dicks from 3rd to 2nd Line -do-	
	11th	Question of Horse Return gone into and noted for future guidance that cast horses etc., must not be included in the Return. Peat Moss in lieu of straw for bedding for Hut Stables to be issued whenever possible.	

Army Form C. 2118.

WAR DIARY
or
INTELLIGENCE SUMMARY
(Sheet 3.)

(Erase heading not required.)

Instructions regarding War Diaries and Intelligence Summaries are contained in F. S. Regs., Part II. and the Staff Manual respectively. Title pages will be prepared in manuscript.

Hour, Date, Place	Summary of Events and Information	Remarks and references to Appendices
November 11th (Ctd.)	G.O.C. inspected 181st Infantry Brigade. Officer reinforcement, 2/20th London Regt proceeds Southampton.	
12th	Dr.Garth Eager appointed Civil Medical Practitioner. 2/5th R.F.A.Brigade moved from Stansted Camp to Billets at Stansted. This Division now comes under War Establishments Part IX for all purposes except promotions.	
13th	Capt.Moss appointed Divisional Remount Officer. £150 paid by Command Paymaster to Hedham R.D.U. to induce them to proceed with Scavenging contracts. 31 G.S. Wagons arrived for distribution.	
14th	Major Campbell, 2/13th London Regt. required to join 1/20th London Regt. as Senior Major. Draft of 27 Drivers required from 2/6th R.F.A.Brigade.	
15th	All Units to hand indent for lamps for night marching. G.O.C. inspected 179th Infantry Brigade. Limbered wagons exchanged for G.S.Wagons.	
16th	Orders received that strength of Infantry Battalions in Officers reduced to 23. Lt.Col.Henriques, C.R.E. and Capt. Ferguson, R.E. proceeded to Esher on duty (returning on completion.)	
17th	O.C.Units directed to immediately report to the Divisional Remount Officer and this office when horses are sold, destroyed etc., and to be struck off Returns rendered to this office. Conducting Officer asked for for draft from 2/6th Brigade R.F.A. Detention rooms at Braintree closed owing to outbreak of Scarlet Fever till November 26th. Inmates and Staff isolated till November 26th. The following transfer is approved, 2/Lt. F.L.White, 2/17th London Regt to 3rd line Unit. Rev.J.C.A.Bohn, Congregationalist, left the Division for service overseas.	
18th	The Saracens Head Public House, Bps. Stortford is placed out of bounds to all Troops of H.M.Forces. G.O.C. inspected R.E., R.A.M.C. and A.S.C Units. Third Army notified us that maze must no longer be regarded as an equivalent for oats and no exchanges to take place.	

Nov. 13?: 6300 303 Rifles ammunition to be received by this General in exchange for all Jap Rifles thereof.
1,890,000 rounds of .303 ammunition to be received in exchange for Jap ammunition thereof.

1247 W 3299 200,000 (E) 8/14 J.B.C. & A. Forms/C. 2118/11.

Army Form C. 2118.

WAR DIARY
or
INTELLIGENCE SUMMARY. (Sheet 4.)
(Erase heading not required.)

Instructions regarding War Diaries and Intelligence Summaries are contained in F.S. Regs., Part II. and the Staff Manual respectively. Title pages will be prepared in manuscript.

Hour, Date, Place	Summary of Events and Information	Remarks and references to Appendices
November 19th.	Col. Butler appointed C.R.A (Third army letter 3459/AQ., 18/11/15. Third Army Signal Coy to be rationed by us as from 14.10.15, as per instructions received from Third Army.	
20th	24 G.S. Wagons arrived for distribution. Lieut. Wetmough, A.O.D. appointed D.A.D.O.S. reports for duty. Attention drawn to Central Force Orders 420,537,981 and 1418, that Officers are not to draw lodging or Fuel and Light Allowance but are to be billeted.	
21st	Central Force Officers inspected 180th Infantry Brigade.	
22nd	A.S.C. notified that in future the R.A.M.C. Transport would be under their Command. Central Force Officers inspected R.F.A. Brigade. 60th (London) Divl. Casualty Clearing removed from Blythwood Camp, Stansted to Elsenham Hall, Elsenham. Col. H.H. Butler reported for duty as C.R.A. Col. H. Weir relinquishes appointment as C.R.A. and is struck off strength. Third army stated that Rock and Common Salt to be indented for when required and 3 lbs. pest Moss would in future be regarded as an equivalent to 1 lb. of Oats.	
23rd	Capt. Horlick, Coldstream Guards, appointed Brigade Major, 181st Infantry Brigade. Report asked for on all Home Service men employed with 2nd Line.	
24th	Capt. Moss takes over duties as Divisional Remount Officer. Investigation made at the instigation of the Third Army of the question of Pte. Bowyer, Yeomanry, not receiving clothing to which he was entitled.	
25th	Rev. J. Sheehan appointed R.C. Chaplain.	
26th	40 Limbered Wagons sent to Tunbridge Wells. Report asked for from higher authority as to condition of roads to Hutments. Issue of Aldershot Ovens and Soyer Stoves sanctioned in lieu of Field Kitchens. 40 Limbered Wagons sent to Tunbridge Wells.	
27th	Units notified they will inform Divisional Remount Officer stating class of horses cast.	
29th	2/15th London Regiment leave Bishops Stortford for Ware. 2/20th London Regt. ordered to proceed to Hertford from Saffron Walden on 2/12/15.	
30th	Machine Gun Sections of 2/13th and 2/15th London Regiments ordered to return to Bps. Stortford. Four Officers required as reinforcements from 2/2nd Co. of Ldn. Yeomanry. Monthly Return asked for from all Units of Troops supplied and accommodated within the Division.	

Army Form C. 2118.

WAR DIARY

INTELLIGENCE SUMMARY.

(Erase heading not required.)

Instructions regarding War Diaries and Intelligence Summaries are contained in F.S. Regs., Part II. and the Staff Manual respectively. Title pages will be prepared in manuscript.

Hour, Date, Place	Summary of Events and Information	Remarks and references to Appendices
2nd December, 1915.	Three Officers, reinforcements, Yeomanry, ordered to be in readiness to proceed overseas. 2/20th Battalion, London Regiment, moved from SAFFRON WALDEN to HAVERHILL. A.A. & Q.M.G. (in G.O.C's absence) inspected billets of R.A. and 2/15th Battalion, London Regiment. Rev. W.J. HOUSE (C.E.) appointed Chaplain as from 7th November, 1915.	
3rd December, 1915.	Rev. J.E. ANDERSON appointed C.E. Chaplain. Courts of Enquiry assembled to enquire into loss of arms and ammunition in charge of various Units of the 179th and 181st Brigades. Rev. C.W. WOOTTON (C.E.) appointed Temporary Chaplain.	
5th December, 1915.	Ordered by 3rd Army to transfer one Red Cross Ambulance to Provisional Brigade.	
6th December, 1915.	Colonel REEVE, Central Force, inspected Mobile Veterinary Section. King George V. Public House, SAWBRIDGEWORTH, placed "out of bounds" to all H.M. Troops. Attention of all Officers was again directed to order regarding Officers visiting Garrison Towns reporting themselves at Headquarters. Lieut. TUCKER, D.A.D.O.S., having proceeded overseas, is struck off strength of Division.	
7th December, 1915.	Captain J. HORLICK, Coldstream Guards, reported for duty as Brigade Major of 181st Brigade. Lieut. Colonel NASH, Royal Scots, reported on attachment, and is posted to 181st Infantry Brigade for duty. Rev. J. SHEEHAN (R.C.) appointed Temporary Chaplain.	

Army Form C. 2118.

WAR DIARY
or
INTELLIGENCE SUMMARY.
(Erase heading not required.)

Instructions regarding War Diaries and Intelligence Summaries are contained in F. S. Regs., Part II. and the Staff Manual respectively. Title pages will be prepared in manuscript.

Hour, Date, Place	Summary of Events and Information	Remarks and references to Appendices
8th December, 1915.	Rev. J.H. JACKMAN (United Board) reported for duty as Temporary Chaplain, and is taken on the strength of the Division from 4th December.	
	Lieut. Colonel & Hon. Colonel H.S. GOLDICOTT, 2/21st Battalion, London Regiment, is transferred from 2nd to 3rd Line Depot. (Authority:- London District Order 14, 7/12/15).	
	Captain COLMAR, 2/22nd Battalion, London Regiment, required at 3rd Army for instruction in Q.M.G. Branch.	
	Recommendation forwarded to London District that Major ROBINSON, 2/16th Battalion, London Regiment, be appointed O.C. 3rd Line. Central Force enquired number of 18 pdr. Guns in possession. Information supplied.	
9th December, 1915.	Instructions issued to all Units re necessity of chain of responsibility through all ranks.	
11th December, 1915.	Field Bakery, Field Butchery, and Depot Units of Supply arrived, and are attached to the Division.	
	Rev. C.W. WOOTTON (C.E.) reported for duty as Temporary Chaplain.	
12th December, 1915.	Lieut. J.A. BARCLAY, 2/16th Battalion, London Regiment, recommended to 3rd Army as 2nd A.D.C.	
	Cyclist Company reported accident to Army aeroplane.	
14th December, 1915.	Recommendation forwarded to London District that Lieut. Colonel BRINCKMAN, 2/22nd Battalion, London Regiment, be appointed O.C. 3rd Line.	
	3rd Army refuse to recommend appointment of Rev. MACPHERSON as Presbyterian Chaplain.	
	Noted in Orders that Rev. R.E. GOODCHILD performed duty as Officiating Clergymen to C. of E. Troops, under Article 406 Royal Warrant, from 1st October to 5th December, 1915.	

WAR DIARY
or
INTELLIGENCE SUMMARY.
(Erase heading not required.)

Army Form C. 2118.

Instructions regarding War Diaries and Intelligence Summaries are contained in F. S. Regs., Part II. and the Staff Manual respectively. Title pages will be prepared in manuscript.

Hour, Date, Place	Summary of Events and Information	Remarks and references to Appendices
15th December, 1915.	Confidential Circular Memo from Central Force dated 8th December, circulated to all Units, regarding correspondence direct with the War Office.	
16th December, 1915.	3rd Army applied for services of Major MILLER, D.A.D.M.S., at EASTON LODGE.	
17th December, 1915.	Recommendation forwarded to London District to appoint Lieut. YOUNG Brigade Machine Gun Officer, 179th Infantry Brigade.	
18th December, 1915.	Application to appoint Lieut. BARCLAY as 2nd A.D.C. refused. Recommendation to appoint Major FLETCHER to command 2/21st Battalion forwarded. 3rd Army approve of proposal of Signal Company to use flash lamps at night. Instructions received by Infantry Battalions from Central Force to despatch Officers in excess of 23 to 3rd Line.	
19th December, 1915.	Major-General E.S. BULFIN, C.V.O., C.B., assumed Command of the Division. GOSFIELD placed "out of bounds" by A.D.M.S.	
20th December, 1915.	------	
21st December, 1915.	Central Force called for an immediate report from all Units as to whether they would be fit for service overseas.	
22nd December, 1915.	------	
23rd December, 1915.	Orders received from 3rd Army that Officers of Howitzer Brigade were to be recalled for duty with Brigade.	

Army Form C. 2118.

WAR DIARY
or
INTELLIGENCE SUMMARY.
(Erase heading not required.)

Instructions regarding War Diaries and Intelligence Summaries are contained in F.S. Regs., Part II. and the Staff Manual respectively. Title pages will be prepared in manuscript.

Hour, Date, Place	Summary of Events and Information	Remarks and references to Appendices
24th December, 1915.	Recommendation forwarded to 3rd Army for appointment of Major FEGEN as D.A.D.M.S.	
	Christmas message received from H.M. THE KING. Special Order issued.	M
	Orders issued to all Units on the subject of Responsibility.	M
	War Office letter issued to all Units on the subject of Illegal Signalling Apparatus.	M
25th December, 1915.	--------	
26th December, 1915.	--------	
27th December, 1915.	Senior Officers from Infantry, R.E., R.A., and A.S.C. proceeded to France for short tour of instruction.	
	Orders received from 3rd Army that Battalions will be brought up to War Establishment.	M
28th December, 1915.	Report sent to 3rd Army re impossibility of sending personnel to R.E. Training Depot, CIRENCESTER.	M
29th December, 1915.	W.O. letter received giving minimum establishment of Officers of Units of Divisional Troops.	M
30th December, 1915.	Orders received that Divisional Ammunition Column was to be raised.	M
31st December, 1915.	Ruling received from 3rd Army that strength of Officers will be increased from 23 per Battalion, proportionate to men.	
	3rd Army call for Departmental reports on matters affecting efficiency of the Division. - Forwarded.	

B. Stokes
5.1.1916

[signature]
AA&QMG

www.ingramcontent.com/pod-product-compliance
Lightning Source LLC
Chambersburg PA
CBHW081517160426
43193CB00014B/2714